ISFJ:

Understand And Break Free From Your Own Limitations

MATTHEW BRIGHTHOUSE

Copyright © 2017

Table of Contents

Introduction

If you have taken the Myers-Briggs Personality Test and you have come up as an ISFJ personality type, you are someone who is very special indeed. You are 'The Defender'.

Whilst your type make up approximately 13% of the overall population, you are within a group of people who love to do good work, who take great pride in helping others, and who will strive to assist someone else, even if it means putting themselves second.

This book is going to help you understand your ISFJ personality type, and allow you to learn more about what makes you tick. Of course, it is unlikely that you are 100% ISFJ, and it could be that you display traits of surrounding personality types. This is a very common scenario, because none of us really ever fit into a box with set rules. If this is the case, it's a good idea to read up on the other types which you are displaying the traits of, and then you can really help yourself become a well-rounded individual.

For now however, we're talking about ISFJs alone.

You are in good company in this bracket, as celebrities such as Beyoncé, Halle Berry, and Vin Diesel are all ISFJs, but it is also likely that anyone you meet who is very keen to help others, e.g. nurses, charitable workers, etc, has a strong ISFJ presence in their make-up.

This is because ISFJs are sensitive to the needs and wants of others. We will talk about this particular issue in great detail later, but overall, the downside means that you are probably likely to be someone who puts themselves second as a result of this. There is nothing wrong with helping others, in fact that is a wonderful quality to have, but it is important not to do this at the detriment of yourself all the time.

Don't worry however, we're going to do a full chapter on this, to help you recognise when you are doing it, and learn how to correct it, before it becomes a big problem in your life.

Because of your ISFJ sensitive nature, it is important not to take any of the advice we give you to heart. It is meant to be there to help you, not to criticise you. You don't have any terrible personality traits in this type, you're not someone who is vindictive, you're not nasty, and you're not uncaring, you're actually the total opposite. Of course, that doesn't mean that you don't exhibit some of these traits at some point in your life, because we're all human and do such things occasionally, but overall, you are a caring, helpful, and empathic person, and for that you should give yourself a pat on the back!

So, what can you expect from this book?

We are going to examine what your personality type means, what it is, and what it stands for. We're going to celebrate your strengths, and we're going to explain your weaknesses. Once we know what the weaknesses are, we're going to give you helpful guidance and advice on how to turn those weaknesses into positives, to help you become a truly complete person. You will be able to deal with any of the problems that ISFJ personality types have in the common run of things, because of the advice we give you.

So, without further ado, let's talk about ISFJs and start our journey together.

1
The Fine Line Between Strength and Weakness

Okay, let's talk all about what it means to be an ISFJ, your strengths, your weaknesses, and where we can go from there.

First things first, you'll probably want to know what ISFJ stands for.

- I – Introverted
- S – Sensing
- F – Feeling
- J – Judging

Let's talk about each one in turn, to help you understand what it means to be an ISFJ.

Introverted
You are not someone who is 'out there', and you are not in anyone's face; instead you are someone who is quiet, considerate, and someone who prefers to listen and act, than speak and act. You are someone who works behind the scenes, but you do that tirelessly, often to your own extremes. Shyness comes quite naturally to an ISFJ, and that is something you need to work on and learn to conquer. Again, don't worry, we're going to talk about that a little later on.

Sensing

You are very intuitive, and you can sense someone's need for help. This is because you are very empathic in many ways, and your sensitivity can be either about yourself and your feelings, or it can be about the feelings of others. It is no bad thing to be sensitive to the feelings and problems of someone else, and this is one of the key factors of why you are always so keen to help out someone else. Ironically however, you have a tendency to repress certain feelings of your own.

Feeling

Because you are an introvert and because you have that sensing quality, you are someone who acts on feelings. Having said that, you are quite a contradiction, because as an ISFJ, you have a very logical mind too, and you can use your feeling sense to act on not only sensitivities to emotions, but using your brain to figure out the best way to deal with something. This is quite a powerful combination.

Judging

Your powerful, logical, mind does have a tendency to make you judgmental from time to time, but this is only to a small degree. You actually use your judgement to great use in other situations in your life, although you are a little resistant to change by your nature. If you can learn to go with the flow a little, and be a little less resistant to the changes that life brings you, then you will be putting yourself in a good position.

So, now we know what ISFJ stands for, and we know that you're a pretty charitable and helpful kind of person, but let's explore it in a bit more depth and look at your strengths, and then your weaknesses.

ISFJ Strengths

It's always good to talk about plus points before we get onto perceived negatives, so let's talk about your upsides.

Supportive
You are a great friend and supporter, and if someone needs a cheerleader in their corner, you're a great person to choose. You love to build people up, you're never someone who loves to knock others down, and this means you will always support and hold someone's hand through a problem. If someone is lacking in confidence about something, you're the person who boost them up, and you're a fantastic friend overall.

This sometimes does mean that you support others and give them your attention when you should be really focusing on yourself, but in terms of downsides, it's not exactly a major negative! If you can learn to give yourself more time and put yourself first a little more (we'll talk about that later), you can continue to be that amazing supporter and friend, whilst allowing yourself to flourish too.

Always Empathise, Rather Than Judge
You are very sensitive to the feelings of others, and you always empathise and sympathise, before you judge. You're can be judgemental occasionally, but this is not something that happens often. You are much more likely to look past someone's actions, and

look into why they did it instead. Of course, this sometimes means that you give someone the benefit of the doubt for their actions when you really shouldn't have, but we know what they say about karma ....

Patient

You are actually quite a patient person, and you will wait for the right moment, rather than rushing into something. Of course, this doesn't mean that from time to time you don't jump feet first into something because you're excited, but overall, and especially in work, you're a patient individual.

Reliable

As well as being patient, you're super reliable. At work, you are the first person someone goes to when they need a job deadline to be met. You always do exactly what you say you're going to do, and you never let people down. If by some strange reason you have to let someone down, through no fault of your own, you have a habit of feeling a little upset about it for a while. It's fine to say 'no' sometimes, and this is something we're going to talk about in much more detail later on.

Imaginative

You have a fantastic creative mind, and that means you can come up with solutions to problems with ease. Ironically, you have a great logical mind too, which means your solutions are likely to work! It's no surprise that many charitable workers are ISFJ personality types, and when it comes to fund raising ideas, the more creative and outrageous, the better! ISFJs find it easy to come up with these ideas.

Loyal

We have already mentioned that you're a great supporter and friend, and that is partly because you are super-loyal. You will not let someone down, and you will never betray them easily. You do what you say you're going to do, and you take it super-personally if someone lets you down or doesn't meet their obligations. This is because you would never do the same to them.

Hardworking

As you are loyal and reliable, you are very hardworking too. You will, as we mentioned, always strive to meet your deadlines, but this also means you are likely to tire yourself out in the process. It's fine to ask for help sometimes, and it's also more than fine to say 'no' too.

ISFJ Weaknesses

Okay, now we know all your upsides, and you have a lot, quite a few more than some other personality types can claim to have. Let's talk about your weaknesses now. As we mentioned earlier, don't take this as a criticism, and see it as a tool for growth. The whole point of learning about your personality is to understand where you can learn and improve.

A Little Too Humble Occasionally

There is nothing wrong with being humble, in fact it is a very enviable and lovable trait, but there is a line, and as an ISFJ you have a habit of going over it. Being too humble means you downplay yourself, and you don't give yourself credit for your talents and the positive actions you do in life. Try and learn to pat yourself on the back occasionally – you deserve it! You do lots of wonderful things for other people, and that means you deserve to give yourself credit for it all. The next time someone gives you a compliment for something you did, instead of going 'oh it was nothing really', say 'thank you' and smile. Take the compliment!

Shy
Not every single ISFJ is a shy person, because many of your personality type are very comfortable socially. There is likely to be at least one situation in your life where you are quite shy, be it romance or something else. Shyness can be crippling when it goes too far, and it can stop you from going out and doing great things in your life. Of course, it's not as simple as just saying 'stop being shy', and it is something to work on over time, taking baby steps. It can be done however, and many people who have a natural shyness learn how to conquer it. Despite all that, if your shyness is very minimal, and doesn't affect your life too much, it can actually be an attractive trait.

A Tendency to Put Yourself Second
Earlier on we talked about the fact you are very humble, and that means that you put yourself down in order to build other people up. To go hand in hand with that, you have a tendency to put yourself second. This means that you will allow your own needs and desires to go unmet, in order to have someone else's needs ticked off the list. This isn't always the right way to be, because you are important too. It's all about balance, and learning to put yourself first occasionally (not all the time) will mean you can

achieve that balance in your life, without upsetting yourself or anyone else too.

Repressing Feelings

All of these ISFJ weaknesses are interlinked in many ways. When you downplay yourself and you put yourself second, you begin to repress the way you feel. You don't consider your feelings to be valid, when that is really not the case. If you can learn to own your feelings and recognise that they are just as valid and real as those people you're trying to help, then you will achieve balance once more. It's also the case that repressing the way your feel is actually an unhealthy habit. If you push everything down and keep it bottled up inside, you're never venting or getting everything out in the open. Learn to be more open and accepting of how you feel and you're on the fast track to completeness.

Taking on Too Much

Another linked weakness! ISFJs tend to take on too much work or responsibility, simply because they won't want to hurt anyone's feelings by saying 'no'. The ironic thing about all of this is that if you take on too much, you're not going to be able to tick it all off your list, and you will set yourself up for failure unwittingly. This means you're going to feel bad about yourself, put excessive pressure on yourself, and it all turns into a rather nasty circle that you don't need to be involved in. Learn to say 'no' when you don't want to do something, or simply can't do something.

A Reluctance to Embrace Change

ISFJs don't really love change that much, and the thought of change can cause unnecessary stress. Try and learn how to embrace the fact that change happens, and that most of the time change is good. Change leads to bigger and better opportunities, and that means that if you can simply learn to go with the flow and keep your mind open, you will be in a much better position to accept the great things that will come your way. Of course, letting go of the past is hard for everyone, but the mind-set that change has to happen in order for growth to occur, is the only way through it.

"The only thing that is constant is change"
-Heraclitus

So, there we have it. As you can see, there are more strengths than weaknesses, and that's a major positive to take away. You are a caring, empathic person and for that you should be congratulated. The weaknesses we have mentioned can all be worked on, and that is the main purpose of this book.

Now you know what you need to work on, you have the power to begin. So, without further ado, let's start with our first step towards personality completeness.

2
Learn to Say 'no', And Don't Overload Yourself

One of the biggest weaknesses of an ISFJ is the tendency towards simply doing too much. You want to help out and you do that selflessly, to the point where you overload yourself with everyone else's tasks. This leaves you stressed out, burnt out, and tired.

This tendency also leaves you open to the manipulative grip of people who aren't as selfless as you, and who will simply throw everything at you and take credit for it when it's done. For instance, at work, you may find someone gives you all the hard work to do, e.g. the tasks that no one else wants, but when they are done, and you've done it brilliantly (as always), they take the credit and thanks for it. This leaves you feeling a little resentful, but because you are kind hearted and generous, you keep your mouth closed, to avoid causing a problem. Does this sound familiar to you?

Basically, don't be a doormat. This is easier said than done in many ways, because you don't see it that way. You see it as you helping someone, and there is never any downside to that. The thing is, you need to pick your battles wisely, and only help the people who really need it. That person at work who gives you all the awkward tasks to do, simply because they don't want to do it themselves, they don't really need helping. This is not a cause you should be putting your time and effort into. This is simply a selfish and cynical person who is manipulating your good nature for their own benefit and gain. Wanting to help others is always an exceptional quality, so well done you. Just be aware of certain types of people who make take advantage of your awesome traits.

It is not a failing to say 'no', and it's not wrong to do so either. Obviously, there are situations when you can't say 'no', e.g. when your boss delegates a task to you that is definitely within your work remit and is vitally important. You can explain that you have work to do already, but you will probably simply be told to prioritise and get the job done. That's fine, we all have to do this sometimes in our lives. But, the difference between that situation and one whereby someone is simply giving you work for the sheer hell of it, is that you are totally within your rights to be unhappy about it.

Of course, there is a way to do it. You don't simply go around refusing to do everything because you don't want to, and that's not in your nature anyway. What you need to do is assess every request for help on its merits, and assess it against what you already have on your plate. If it is doable, and if you want to do it, then go for it; if it isn't doable, or basically you just don't want to do it, then say 'no'. Explain kindly that you really wish you could help but that you just don't have the time or capacity at the moment. You could say that if they are really struggling in a few days, you could re-evaluate the situation, but currently it's just not possible.

There is nothing rude about that, it is simply you being kind and true to yourself, as you should be at all times.

Now, we can totally appreciate that as an ISFJ you will find this hard to do, especially the first few times. You're likely to feel pretty bad afterwards, and you'll wonder whether you did the right thing. Do not go back on your decision – you did what you felt and you stood up for yourself too. Leave it at that. People will also respect your work boundaries much more, and stop piling excessive loads onto you if you say 'no' a few times.

This isn't just about work. Because of your empathic and supportive nature, people tend to flock to you for emotional support too. You are loyal and you are not a judgemental person from the get-go, choosing empathy as your first port of call. Now, when someone, or more than one person, constantly loads their problems onto you, even if you are just being a shoulder to cry on, it can tend to drag you down over time. You are not an empath per se, but you do feel bad for those who are struggling, and you may find that you start to feel a little low as a result.

That person doesn't mean to do this to you, they don't even realise they're doing it; they are simply coming to you for help because they know you're such a great supporter. The thing is, when it starts to drag you down too, what do you do?

This is a difficult one, because it is not in your nature at all to turn someone away who really needs help. In this case you need to limit your exposure to this issue, to limit the amount of effect it has on you. In this regard, you're not refusing to help, you're simply not going to be there as their listening ear 24 hours per day. This is compromise, and this is how you manage emotional situations, whilst still being there for that person who needs your help.

Be Your Own Superhero, Not Everyone Else's

Neglecting your own needs for downtime and relaxation is something you need to be cautious of. You are always there for others, as we have mentioned, but sometimes you need to be your own superhero too. Look at it this way – you can't help others if you're not in top shape yourself. You owe it to those you're helping, as well as yourself, to be kind to number one.

This is not being selfish – so get that thought out of your mind! As an ISFJ that is sure to be something that just popped into your head! You are not an endless supply of support for everyone else, you need to support yourself too.

How do you feel about that? How does it make you feel to know that it's totally okay to say 'no' and that you can choose yourself over others occasionally? We're not expecting you to say 'no' to everything, and we're not expecting you to never put someone before yourself, but it's about management, and it's about balance. Be a set of weighing scales, and aim to be in the middle.

3
Learn to Accept That Your Best is Good Enough

Are you ever happy with what you do? Or, more likely, do you push yourself to perfection, to the point where your meticulous nature makes you exhausted?

That is a good description of an ISFJ.

The thing is, whilst you're doing your best and you're working hard, getting everything right, are you taking credit for it? Most ISFJs don't like to shout from the roof tops when they do something great, and they are more likely to allow someone else to take the credit, or simply allow it to 'be', without owning up to it.

You're selling yourself short!

Your best is good enough, your best is MORE than good enough.

Do you always compare what you do to someone else? That's likely too. Because you want to get it right, and because you want to help others with what you do, you're likely to struggle with this point.

ISFJs are likely to be found in jobs that are linked to helping others and those which have history attached to them. For instance, charitable work, teachers, nurses, doctors, basically those who do a job to help other people. You are a nurturer; you want others to do well because it gives you a sense of achievement. In a lot of ways, their achievement is your own credit.

Never underplay your own achievements in life. You have worked hard, and you should allow yourself the credit and praise that you deserve. Yes, you don't want to be screaming from the rooftops 'look what I did', but you know what? If you do something amazing one time, something really amazing, that you're super proud of, why not shout about it? Post it all over your Facebook if you want, because you deserve someone to pat you on the back for everything you do.

ISFJs are quite the contradiction in a lot of ways; you're socially comfortable, and you like people, but you're shy at the same time. You love to do good work, but you don't always like to be in the spotlight to claim the rewards. Yes, Mr or Mrs ISFJ, you are a complicated type!

Put simply, you just need to ask yourself a question at the end of every day – did I do my best?

If the answer to that is 'yes', then you have succeeded in your day and you can turn the page on today's chapter. If the answer is 'could have done better', then you need to ask yourself whether that is really the case at all. ISFJs work hard, so it's unlikely that you could have done much better than you did. If you genuinely could have done better, it's fine, admit it to yourself and move on. Vow to make tomorrow better.

You can't turn back time, you can only make tomorrow more successful, and that's something you need to come to terms with and accept.

The hardest pill for an ISFJ to swallow is when they try and help someone, and it doesn't work. You're not Mother Theresa or Florence Nightingale (or the male version if that counts), but you are super-kind and want to help, so when it doesn't work out, you take it a little personally. You are not responsible for the actions of others. If they don't want your help, you can't force them to take it; if they choose a different option, you tried your best.

It doesn't always work out, and you need to really accept that fact in order to be at peace with yourself.

You're not a person who is lacking confidence per se, you just don't really want to shout it out when you do something. It's not a case that you're a personality type who takes it personally to the point of upset when you don't succeed, but you are someone who beats yourself up internally when you could have helped someone more. Basically, as long as you did your best, you need to understand that you couldn't have done anymore. Because really, ISFJ, your best is often better than most other people's.

4
Learn to Congratulate Yourself

We did touch upon this a little in our last chapter, but this is a big issue for ISFJs, so we need to cover it in more detail in a separate development chapter.

So far, this is what we know about you as an ISFJ:

- You are hard working
- You are honest
- You are patient
- You are kind
- You are nurturing and supportive
- You are enthusiastic
- You choose to be sympathetic, rather than judge

Is any of that bad? No!

So, why are you so hard on yourself?

We are not saying that your personality type is selfish, judgemental, cold, harsh, or vindictive, we are painting a glowing and helpful picture that you should be proud of, and something which you should celebrate. What you do need to work on however, is your tendency to avoid ownership of projects that have gone really well.

We mentioned in our last chapter that you don't like to shout it from the rooftops, but instead you'll let someone else take the credit. Why should that person get your credit? And that's because it is YOURS, not theirs.

Your need to help others means that those unscrupulous types will take your kind nature for granted and use you to get a job done, without them actually putting in any of the hard work. You need to start claiming back that credit and saying 'look what I did!'.

You don't find taking compliments that easy, so let's look at how you can start to try and learn.

How to Take a Compliment

If someone says 'hey that work you did for me yesterday, well done, that was really great', what do you do and say? Do you say 'oh thank you, I really appreciate it?'

That's not likely to be the right answer for an ISFJ.

An ISFJ will instead say 'aw it was nothing', or give the credit to another person in the team.

The thing for you to develop here is the ability to own that compliment, listen to it, and believe it.

So, this is what you should do.

The next time someone says 'well done' to you, you nod your head, smile, and say 'thank you'. If you don't feel like doing that, or you don't really believe it, perhaps it goes totally against the grain, it doesn't matter – fake it. Faking confidence is something that works, so faking the ability to take a compliment is something that works too! It isn't going to happen overnight, and you're not going to be owning compliments left, right, and centre straightaway, but over time, you will notice that your ability to take the compliment in a dignified and understated way develops, and as a result, so will your confidence.

The fact that you are taking pride in your ability and owning it also means that you are going to be less at risk of those people taking credit for your work, or piling too much onto you. They can't take the credit falsely, if you're owning it!

There is a Big Difference Between Confidence and Arrogance

You're not one of those people who like to be around others who blow their own trumpet. You prefer to be around quieter people, those who are confident in their own skin, but don't feel the need to shout about it. This is what you aim to be.

Arrogance is not an attractive quality, and as an ISFJ, you're not likely to ever reach levels of arrogance in your life. Never be afraid to be confident however, because it isn't going to be misconstrued for arrogance if you do it the right way.

Arrogance is shouting, it is being in people's faces, it is generally being boastful about your ability. Arrogant people don't tend to be introverted like you, and they aren't the type of people to go around helping others, like you do. Don't feel that just because you're starting to take credit for your good work, and that you're learning how to accept compliments, that it means you're turning into Mr or Arrogant. Quite the opposite.

You might feel that these 'learn to' chapters are all quite closely linked, and that's no surprise. Most of the weaknesses associated with the ISFJ personality type are literally linked together like a chain. The thing is, you need to treat each link individually, in order to get to the unravelling stage.

Let's move on to the next one.

5
Learn to Put Yourself First

Overloading yourself is a form of not putting yourself first. Not saying 'no' when you really want to or need to, is a form of not putting yourself first. Not taking credit for your achievements and good work, is another form of not putting yourself first.

Can you see where we're going with this?

We mentioned in one of our previous chapters that if you don't look after yourself and don't ensure you're in the best shape, that you can't look after anyone else, or help them either. Think about Beyoncé for example, she is an ISFJ too. Beyoncé does a lot for charity and helping others, she is a pioneer of music and she gives advice and guidance through her songs. Whilst Beyoncé is not someone who shouts from the rooftops 'look at me, I'm amazing', at least not when she is off stage and out of character, she is someone who is quietly confident and assured in herself.

Why do you think this is?

Because she has learnt the importance of putting herself first on occasion.

Beyoncé is a mother, and she knows that as a mother, she cannot be the best nurturer for her children unless she is happy and heathy herself. To that aim, she works out, she eats healthily, she makes time for herself, and she pours her creativity into her job. This means that she is putting herself first, enabling her to be there for her children, her fans, and her friends.

Can you see what we're getting at?

You need to nurture yourself as you would nurture the person you're trying to help.

You need to eat healthily, you need to exercise, you need to make sure you get the right amount of sleep, you need to learn to say 'no' firmly but politely when you don't have the time to do something, and you need to learn that it's okay to do all of those things FOR YOU.

You were not put on this earth for everyone else, you were put on this earth to live your life, and touch the lives of others as you go through your years on this planet. And by being the best version of yourself, you will be able to have the greatest impact on others too.

How do You Put Yourself First?

You might be wondering how on earth you actually achieve this putting yourself first business. We just talked about eating and sleeping property, but is that all it is about?

No.

Putting yourself first is about knowing your limitations as a person, nurturing your own health and wellbeing, and understanding that your own mental and emotional health has to come first. Again, we will say it, you cannot help others if you are not helping yourself.

Do we sound like a stuck record yet?

Your Emotions Matter

One of the main weaknesses of an ISFJ is a tendency towards repressing emotions and feelings. If you keep everything bottled up, you're not going to be healthy on the inside. How can you be healthy on the outside in that case?

A key reason that ISFJs keep their emotions dampened down is because they think (wrongly) that they need to be strong for other people, and that they haven't got the time or support to have their own emotional issues.

This is unfair on you, because you are a human being, so of course there are going to be times when you feel down, or when you simply want to offload your problems or feelings onto someone else. This is a totally normal human trait to have, and you need to have the support network and ability to be able to do just that.

So, how can you allow your emotions to flow more freely?

The ironic thing about this particular subject is that as an ISFJ, you're not emotionally cold, you're actually very emotional, and very sensitive, it's just that you think everyone else is more important than you. In order to value your own emotions and learn that they are just as important as everyone else's, you need to basically let it all out.

Give yourself some 'you' time, have a day off, do the things you love, go out with a friend, basically unwind and don't allow anyone else to unload their baggage on you that particular day. This is your day. If you begin to feel something, or you notice that you're feeling down or upset about something, speak to a friend.

Don't be worried about burdening anyone with your feelings, they're probably going to be very happy to help you out for once, because you're sure to be helping them out all the time. Give them the chance to help you! You will notice that as soon as you have talked about it, you feel instantly lighter, and that is the overall aim.

Repressed feelings are not healthy, and even though you are doing it with the best intentions in your mind, i.e. freeing up your time and emotional capacity for other people, you're actually doing yourself much more harm than good.

When we keep emotions bottled up inside, they can begin to take place in physical pain and illness, including disease. Expression is an extremely important part of living a healthy life.

Let those emotions be free!

6
Learn to Embrace Change

Do you like change?

The expected answer to that is a shake of the head and a 'no'.

Nobody loves it when things change, not if they're really honest. As human beings we like our safety net, we like our comfort blanket, and when that is whipped away quickly, we start to panic, or we begin to feel a little unsettled, or out of sorts. You're not in the minority when you feel this way, you're actually reacting in a totally normal way, but it is helpful to try and embrace change as much as possible.

Change is inevitable, change happens, you can't stop it, so why even try.

Life ebbs and flows, life moves on, life is an endless cycle of change, and with that change come answers and better opportunities. Whilst things might never be entirely the same again, would you really want them to be?

Embracing change can be scary, and if you didn't feel nervous about it then you wouldn't be a human being. It's important to allow that change to occur and not resist it. Resisting change simply creates stress, and you don't need that in your life.

When a change happens it can be instant, or you can know about it beforehand. Which is better? In a lot of ways it is better for change to occur out of the blue. When this happens, you don't have the time to stress out and work yourself up, overthinking every little detail. When you have prior warning you start to come up with worst case scenarios and that is not useful to anyone.

How to Handle Change

First things first, you need to understand that change happens for a reason. At the time you might not realise what that reason is, but simply know that there is a reason regardless. Change occurs in order for us to grow, and understanding the ever changing circle of life will help you when a situation that requires change occurs.

You might be upset about it, you might not have the first clue how to deal with it, but breathe. You'll get through it. That is something else you need to know in all certainty.

How you deal with it really depends on what the situation is. Is it a personal issue? Is it a break up? Is it a new relationship developing? It is a loss of someone you love? Depending on whether the change is negative or positive depends on how you approach it.

We tend to be more fearful of negative change, although even positive change can come disguised as a negative at first. Firstly, do what we mentioned – accept the change has happened, or is going to happen, and there is nothing you can do to stop it. You should not try and resist change, because if it's meant to happen, it's going to happen regardless of whatever you do.

Next, think about it rationally, when you have calmed down. Is it really as bad as you thought? Is your life going to be over? It's doubtful. Will you survive? You certainly will. Try and think on the positive side – things might be different, but that doesn't mean they're going to be worse, perhaps they'll be better!
Once you've calmed and become a little more rational, grab a pen and paper and brainstorm your thoughts. This

is a good way to get clarity on an issue that is otherwise causing you confusion. Again, once you see it in black and white in front of you, you'll see it's not that scary at all.

Now comes the living with it part. Do not become a martyr or victim of change – be a pioneer! Approach the change in the same way you would approach helping someone in need. We know that as an ISFJ you love to do just that, so open your mind and go fearlessly into the new future that is coming your way.

You'll only have to do this a few times for it to become second nature. The scariest thing about change is the unknown, and once you have flexed the change muscle a few times and noticed it is indeed not that scary, you'll be able to accept and embrace change for the better.

7
Learn to Conquer Your Shyness

Our final 'learn to' chapter is one which is certainly going to take some time to conquer, but it is one which can definitely be done!

We mentioned that ISFJs have a tendency to be very socially comfortable on one hand, but then when a situation is put in front of them, they can become cripplingly shy. One of those situations is matters of the heart.

It's a total contradiction here again, because ISFJs love family and stability, they are at their best when they are feeling loved, happy, and content, and when they are nurturing something or someone else, e.g. a relationship and partner. Long term relationships are the aim for ISFJs, something they all (mostly) want and desire. The thing is, in order to get to the long term relationship part of the deal, you actually have to date someone and see where it goes, open up your entire self to another person and be fearless. ISFJs generally have a bit of a problem with that part.

As you can see, shyness in romance can be a problem for an ISFJ, and a stumbling block towards the thing they want most in life.

Now, if you're reading this and shaking your head, because romance is not on your agenda and you don't have issues with romantic shyness, then examine closely. Are there other areas of your life where shyness affects you? There is likely to be something, whether it is starting a new job, speaking to people you don't know, there will probably be something out there that causes you anxiety in terms of shyness. This is a key feature of an ISFJ.

The problem with shyness is that when left unattended to, it can cause issues in life. It can prevent you from going after what you really want, it can leave you lacking in confidence, as you kick yourself for an opportunity lost. In your mind you were probably itching to speak to that guy or girl at that party, but you found yourself frozen to the spot and now you're left wondering 'what if'. Basically, you should make conquering your shyness the number one priority on your list.

ISFJs generally speaking aren't crippled by shyness in all areas of life, and it is usually romance where it strikes the most. The thing is, if you can just get past that part of it, you really can have what you want, without question.

How to Kick Out Shyness

This is going to be a total fake it until you make it kind of deal. There is no other way around it. During the process of conquering your shyness, you're going to feel uncomfortable, you're going to cringe, and you're going to want to run and hide, but you must see it through. Once you've put yourself out there just one time, you'll see it doesn't cause you physical pain or embarrassment, and you'll find it much easier to do the next time, and the next time, until your shyness is dampened right down.

Most of us experience shyness at some point in our lives, and it's important to realise that there isn't a cure per se. You can conquer your shyness for the most part, but in your future you might encounter another situation where your shyness rears its head again. The positive in that however is that you conquered it once, and you know what to do, so it's entirely possible to kick it out once more.

So, how to conquer it?

The next time you experience a bout of shyness, e.g. anxiety, nerves, you want to run and hide, you simply can't speak to that person, you get shaky, sweaty, you want to do something about it but you just can't move, you're stuck to the spot – breathe. Take yourself mentally out of the situation for just a second and breathe, allow yourself to calm. Close your eyes if you really have to, but relax your mind and body just enough to think rationally.

Now, what is it that you want to do, that your shyness is preventing you from doing? Is it going over to that guy or girl and saying 'hi'? if so, start small. Make eye contact, smile; always remember to smile because it will relax you internally, and it will create the illusion of confidence. We are faking confidence here, remember!

Now, what happened? Did the person run off screaming? Probably not. It is entirely possible that the other person is just as shy as you and was waiting for you to make the first move. If you don't try, you'll never know!

What is the worst that can happen? Ask yourself that next. Nothing is going to happen that you can't survive.

Okay, so now you need to continue to fake your confidence, and you do that by taking a very large breath, stealing yourself for a second, and doing the exact thing which is causing you such anxiety.

Yes, you feel the fear, dear ISFJ, and you jolly well do it anyway.

You will be shaking, you will probably mumble a bit, and you'll probably be sweating, but if you can continue to smile, fake that confidence, you'll eventually begin to feel it too.

You only have to try this once for your confidence to grow, and with every single flex of that confidence muscle yet again, your shyness will be banished to the far reaches of your self conscious mind.

Conquering shyness does not happen overnight, and yes, it's going to take time and effort, but it can be done. Once you win this fight, you will find that doors open; it's almost like the sun coming out from behind a dark cloud, because that's what shyness can feel like sometimes.

As we mentioned at the start of this chapter, the funny thing about the ISFJ personality type is that whilst shyness is an issue, it is not an issue in all parts of life. Most people who suffer from shyness find that it affects them in so many different situations, but for the ISFJ, it is likely to be one particular area only. If you can pinpoint which area that is, you will be able to work on it and conquer the fear.

Conclusion

So there we have it, the confusing and sometimes contradicting world of the ISFJ personality type! Hopefully by this point you will be feeling confident and inspired by the advice we've given you, and you'll be putting it to work on the weakness areas we've explored.

We definitely need to point out once more, as an ISFJ you are a very nurturing and caring individual, someone who is a true helper and defender of others, hence the name The Defender. Aside from that however, you are your own worst enemy in many ways, because that nature of yours, the tendency to not want to refuse to help someone, means that you can easily be taken advantage of. It's really a case of developing your confidence and being aware of this possibility, and from there you can really start to kick out your weaknesses and grow on your strengths.

Be sure to check out the other personality types that you displayed any common traits with, as combining them all together and working as one can help you become a much more well-rounded individual overall. None of us are perfect, and throughout our lives we all develop traits which can be tweaked and changed to create a more balanced experience for ourselves, and for those around us. Never see a weakness as a negative, see it as a chance to grow and learn, an opportunity to change something and make it better.

As an ISFJ you are always helping and supporting others, so maybe it is now time that you put some of that nurturing time and effort into yourself. Ironically, at the same time you're also helping those around you, because by putting more 'me' time into your itinerary, you're strengthening your resolve and ability to aid others too.

So, take credit where credit is due, learn to say 'no', push out that shyness, and learn to let out your emotions – if you can do all of that (entirely doable), then you really have conquered your personality type.

Note from the author

Thank you for purchasing and reading this book. If you enjoyed it or found it useful then I'd really appreciate it if you would post a short review on Amazon. I do read all the reviews personally so that I can continually write what people are wanting.

If you'd like to leave a review then please visit the link below:

https://www.amazon.com/dp/B077S9CLFM

Thanks for your support and good luck!

Check Out My Other Books

Below you'll find some of my other books that are popular on Amazon and Kindle as well. Simply search the titles listed below on Amazon. Alternatively, you can visit my author page on Amazon to see other work done by me.

ENFP: Understand and Break Free From Your Own Limitations

INFP: Understand and Break Free From Your Own Limitations

ENFJ: Understand and Break Free From Your Own Limitations

INFJ: Understand and Break Free From Your Own Limitations

ENFP: INFP: ENFJ: INFJ: Understand and Break Free From Your Own Limitations – The Diplomat Bundle Series

INTP: Understand and Break Free From Your Own Limitations

INTJ: Understand and Break Free From Your Own Limitations

ENTP: Understand and Break Free From Your Own Limitations

ENTJ: Understand and Break Free From Your Own Limitations

<u>ISTJ: Understand and Break Free From Your Own Limitations</u>

<u>OPTION B: F**K IT - How to Finally Take Control Of Your Life And Break Free From All Expectations. Live A Limitless, Fearless, Purpose Driven Life With Ultimate Freedom</u>

www.ingramcontent.com/pod-product-compliance
Lightning Source LLC
Chambersburg PA
CBHW051135250726

48655CB00007B/3081